Basadzi Voices

An anthology of poetic writing by young black
South African women

Compiled by Rose Mokhosi

UNIVERSITY OF KWAZULU-NATAL PRESS

Published in 2006 by University of KwaZulu-Natal Press
Private Bag X01
Scottsville 3209
South Africa
Email: books@ukznpress.ac.za
Website: www.ukznpress.co.za

ISBN: 10: 1-86914-102-4
      13: 978-1-86914-102-8

Editor: Elana Bregin
Layout and design: RockBottom Design
Cover design: Flying Ant Designs
              Sebastien Quevauvilliers

Printed and bound by Interpak Books, Pietermaritzburg

A Word of Thanks

Special thanks go to the members of Young Basadzi Projects, and to friends and family for your generous support, love and patience. And, in particular, to the poets who have enthusiastically contributed to this collection. This dream-book would not have been possible without you.

Thanks also to our rich history, our mothers, fathers and forefathers who led the way, fought the battles and brought us to this point, this time – where we can express ourselves with freedom and celebrate our beautiful African heritage with pride.

And to UKZN Press for giving us this opportunity, and for your endless patience and support.

Acknowledgements

'Bring down the tall walls' was published in *TurfWrite* 2004/2005; 'My people's tongue' in *Pangs of Initiation* (2004); 'The forgotten people' and 'Her name is Limpopo' in *Timbila* 2002 and 2003; 'Take me back North' in *Timbila* 2002 and *Throbbing Ink* 2003; 'The pinnacle of my youth' in *The Golden Thread* and *Angle Search* youth magazine; and 'Like a mad woman catching flies in mid-air' in *Agenda*.

Contents

Compiler's Note

The idea of the *Basadzi Voices* collection was inspired by my love and passion for the arts and born out of a long-cherished dream. This dream began in July 2004, when I started the Young Basadzi poets' group in Durban.* My intention was to give a writing and performance platform specifically to young women, who often find it difficult and intimidating to stand up and perform their poems in public. The dream has encountered many challenges on its way to fruition, and in the course of this long and testing journey I have learnt a lot and grown a lot, both as a poet and a person. Now the dream is a reality! And I am convinced that *Basadzi Voices* has a greater role to play than simply as a poetry showcase. For me, this collection is not just about the art of writing, but empowering women to believe in themselves and their talents.

As young black South African women, we are truly fortunate to have been born into these exciting times. South Africa today, 12 years into democracy, is a country that actively embraces women and their contributions and encourages them to achieve what, previously, they could never even have imagined was possible. This is not to discount the problems of being female in a country with one of the highest gender abuse and AIDS statistics in the world. But, too often, so much focus is given to these negatives that it is easy to overlook the positives of what has been achieved. As women, ours is a path filled with challenges, but also with opportunities and many, many possibilities. The onus is on us to face up to the challenges with courage, grab onto the opportunities with enthusiasm, and use the many possibilities to shape our destinies and make something big of our lives.

* You can find our Young Basadzi weblog at: http://youngbasadzi.blogspot.com

It is in solidarity with other women that we find our strength and inspiration. It is through dialogue and exchange that we are able to share ideas, source solutions and turn our dreams into reality. The arts give a wonderful platform for women to be able to express themselves and utilise their talents in service of the greater cause. Through television programmes, drama, music, art and the like, there has been a lot of exposure of women's issues, and these mediums have become facilitators in highlighting and addressing concerns around rape, AIDS, abuse, marriage, and relationship problems in general. Female artists such as Thandiswa Mazwai, Nkhensani Manganyi and Lebo Mashile are just a few of the many who have been able to exploit their talents positively to make a difference, and in their work the message is clear: 'You are an African woman, so be proud! ANYTHING IS POSSIBLE!'

Basadzi Voices, in a way, encompasses these essential dialogues – of women, between women, about women. The collection was born out of an email I sent out in November 2004, calling for young women writers to submit poems for inclusion in a collection to be called *I Write*, which I was intending to self-publish. The response was overwhelming – 50 poets from around the country replied! This underscored for me the importance of the undertaking. The 13 talented voices represented here have been selected from this original group. They come from all corners of South Africa, and range in age from 19 to 29 years old. Some are students, some are lecturers, secretaries, physiotherapists, accountants, some are travelling the world. Yet, as their poems reveal, they share a surprising similarity of outlook, life experience and concerns.

In this collection they come together to give voice to what is happening in the lives of young South African women right now. Their poems speak from the heart and soul, through print and paper, about the experiences, concerns, passions, hopes, dreams and struggles that affect not only them, but the lives of women generally.

Each of these pieces is not just a self-standing entity but an integral part of the collective whole. They have been loosely grouped into themes according to their subject matter. These range across questions of identity; Africa and belonging; experiences of sexual violation; AIDS and other social ills; love, loneliness and other human emotions; and the quest to find an individual identity that reflects the true soul. The added value of this collection, for me, is that the voices represented here are voices that, until very recently, were forced for reasons of social or cultural pressure to remain mute. Now let out, they speak up with courage and frankness.

It is my hope that this collection will be a source of inspiration to other young South African women, encouraging them to dream big and live out their dreams. In the words of poet Hale Tsehlana, we 'write because it is time' – OUR time!

Rose Mokhosi

Behold Africa

Rose Mokhosi

Your daughter comes to you in all humbleness
on my knees. I ask that you shower me
with your soft rain,
drown me
in the sweet scent of your soil brown.

For those before me
to open doors, and paths to your glory
to your freedom, your embracing arms.
Africa, my mother, my father –
my soul to renounce, to proclaim and to celebrate.
To mourn, to live and to breathe,
to be, to dream and to bring life to your children,
your sons and daughters.

Bring down the tall walls

Phomelelo Machika

Bring down the tall walls
that are supposed to guard my freedom,
yet suffocate the African child that I am.

Bring down the tall walls,
resuscitate my gasping language
which lost breath when the bricks of freedom
were mounted high above my humble beginnings.

Bring down the tall walls,
which have separated me from myself, my people,
burying my inheritance
rendering me a lost child,
although I have a strong bloodline of heroes
boSekhukhune the Great, Maphankgane the Warrior,
the one who scatters burning firewood.

Bring down the tall walls,
immortalise the royalty that I am, my birthright
for I remain the very African child
whose umbilical cord was buried in the landscapes of KwaZulu-Natal
fertilising the land, producing sugarcane.

I am the rightful heir,
who should lay claim to the waters, the mountains
and the glades of the majestic Mpumalanga.

I am the prodigal daughter
returning to claim ownership of Africa's Eden,
Limpopo my wealth.

Bring down the tall walls,
hear them mimic the beat of a drum
with their thunderous fall,
so Africa can remember who she is, for Africa is me.

'Toll gate into Africa' *

Hale Tsehlana

The night was long and cold.
The same dreams came to me,
deep in my sleep,
suffocating inside the mine shaft,
struggling to escape the nightmare;
only to wake up into another.

See the witches hobbling home
on their broken brooms.
The cock signals, the start of another day
like yesterday. The warm sun does nothing
to chase the nightmares away.
I sleepwalk thru the day.

Since I know this land so well,
maybe I will be a land surveyor,
or perhaps a tourist guide,
or own some vast farmland of my own.

I must stop dreaming; another car comes,
perhaps I can make a sale or two.
Let me fetch my clay cows
and the shimmering stones.
Maybe the tourist wants some souvenirs
and may even drop a shilling or two.

---

* Inspired by Ingrid de Kok's poem, 'Road through Lesotho'
  (*Familiar Ground*, Ravan Press, 1988).

  'But there he is before us   His breath grinds dry and hard
  blocking escape   he has three clay oxen for sale.'
  a toll gate into Africa.

My great-grandfather's dream

Dineo Luthuli

I dreamt I was a woman.
Waking up in the morning,
not feeling like bathing nor eating.
Walking forever in this blazing hot sun,
forever in this heatwave.
Walking forever in this snow,
eternally unnoticed in this forever-changing world.
Looking in this mirror yet not recognising this image.
Facing my direction, imagining living in a world of the living.
For in this one I have seen not living souls,
but souls dying from dead dreams, dead goals.
Imagining my mouth flowing with healing waters,
my charisma healing longing and hungry beings.
Healing a common but taboo disease.
Telling, sharing a common but untold story.
Growing, raising, feeding, crusading.
Believing in not dying from unanswered prayers
but praying for answers, living my dream today,
for I may just wake up tomorrow,
need what I've sweated for,
a destiny I may or may not reach.

Broken

Rose Mokhosi

I have never seen a sky
so deep blue-green, soft white cloud floats.
The eagle spreads its wings,
soars high up.
Never seen such tranquility.
For a brief moment it is calm elation.

My body stills to the warmth of the sun,
my spirit lifts up one with the eagle.
We fly free of chains up the mountains,
down the valley and like a vulture drawn to a carcass
we hover over my body amongst the tall yellow
moisture-drawn reeds.

Torrents of tears send me plunging down.
Who is this man on top of me?

His left hand over my mouth, I can not scream.
My eyes blinded, I can not see.
My body numbed, I can not move.
Emotions paralysed, I can not believe.

His right hand groping my breast bruised blue.
Sweat beads on his forehead
trickles down my thigh.
His pants down to his knees,
violently penetrating my most sacred.
Tears deep inside me,
ripping me agape.
Leaving me behind with this broken body.

The mire of womanhood

Hale Tsehlana

What the mire taught me can never be taken away;
it gave me a voice to speak for myself
it opened doors and unleashed pregnant potential
it deepened my understanding of the self
it grew me wings and taught me to say NO.

So when you wear your
hyphenated smile
and try to derail my mind
I've got news for you –
I have my shock absorbers in place
you can't hurt me anymore.

What the mire taught me can never be taken away;
it taught me to sing
and to celebrate myself
it taught me to fly in the face of the wind.
It grew me wings and
taught me to fly.

An unfinished woman

Khanyisile Magubane

I lie here on my back,
sweating, smelling.
Neither woman nor girl, stuck.
Tears roll down the sides of my eyes –
stupid, stupid, stupid me!

Forever has begun,
my sad story has just found its beginning.
I'm cold, freezing.
The window is open,
the thin curtain is blowing inside out
and the cold wind dries me.

I hear cars outside hooting
and angry drivers indulging in road-rage.
To them, I'm just a dimly-lit window –
the silence fools them into ignorance.

I have no energy to scream,
I don't want to scream.
I want a reason, a reason for myself.
A reason to stand 20 years from today.

I am an unfinished woman
with no reason and no cause.
My next step is inside my mind,

to move on far and away from here.
To be free from questions with no answers,
from judgements with no justice,
from stares with no mercy.

I am an unfinished woman.

It must have been love

Neiloe Khunyeli

She swirled around in the darkness and her heart spun like a crack fiend. All she heard was the loud silence. She lay in her own nightmare and felt him ripping her apart.

'I could not help but admire, what's your name Miss Darling? Please give me your number,' he had said with a smile. How could she say no to that smile? So she laughed and agreed to let him buy her dinner.

Some studies estimate that one in two South African women will be raped in their lifetime.[*] A mother will be stripped of her dignity, a sister brutalised and a little girl made a woman in three minutes. Insurance companies now sell rape policies and life gets a little harder even in 'safe' spaces. They bombard us with warning tales about how cruel life can be, but when you have breasts it gets downright impossible.

She was a bit nervous before the first date. It was not every day she let a total stranger take her out, but she had a good feeling about this one. So she took things slowly and he was patient and he promised her the world. The first time they kissed, butterflies took refuge in her stomach. He walked her home and with him she knew she was safe.

Pornography definitely helps to perpetuate the myth that 'no means yes'. The celebration of violence against women within popular culture does not exactly help young girls or boys. In the name of freedom of expression the free world deems it democratic to sing songs that encourage

---

[*] These include studies by the Commission on Gender Equality (1999) and Rape Crisis (1999), based on 1997 police estimates.

the abuse of women; after all, it is just words. The rapist with the smile probably does not even listen to rap or heavy metal, but the mentality is the same.

But now she was alone in the dark and her mind was blank. Her four torn walls were the throbbing reminder of her violation. Sometimes she would scream into the night and damn the whole world. At other times the silence would come and speak to her of blame. She would shake her head to that little voice that whispered, 'You wanted him to do it – you let it happen.'

Studies show that in most cases women are raped by someone they know and trust. It could be a friend, a relative or a colleague. It could also be a date or a boyfriend who romances his way into her trust. Then, one day the flowers, the sweet words and shy kisses end up with her bleeding the 'love' away.

She had firmly said that he must take her home. They had been seeing each other steadily for six months now, and she was uncomfortable with his forceful nature. Tonight she would break it off; she would simply tell him that it was not working out. He was too silent in the car; she could almost feel the rage humming in him.

She never had a chance to explain why she wanted or rather needed out of the relationship. His cold, hard fist slammed into her face before she could explain why. Slowly, the darkness of the night dimmed even more – until she could see nothing.

If he is aggressive and it always takes him a while to stop in his advances after you have asked numerous times, then get away. If he pressurises you about sex all the time even after you have made yourself clear, then get away. If he seems to find nothing wrong with seeing women bruised and battered, then get away. Rapists rarely come with warning signs, so be wary even of the private school brother, or the one who looks like he could be a *GQ* model.

She waited for the spasms to pass and thought about hurting somebody. She remembered his words as he walked away and left her lying there. He had simply shrugged and said: 'It must have been love.'

He was lost in a different way. Cells regenerate and vaginal walls mend, but lost souls are mere specks on Lucifer's playground.

She prayed to be able to get up tomorrow and find her smile.

Seasonal women

shameeyaa neo waMolefe

When the wind blows,
flowers bloom with the eclectic breeze
to welcome the new season.
when the season changes,
trees entwine their leaves to form mosaic patterns
for birds to whistle their tuneless melodies.

when the season changes,
whispering breezes wander through
our mothers' gardens with compassionate sighs,
and butterflies soothe the flowers with their passion.

when the season changes,
shebeens will be filled with barren women
drinking beer in hope of seeing no new day.
prostitutes will parade the streets of Hillbrow
with scarlet g-strings and unwashed bras
selling their bodies from poverty-stricken frustration, while
praying for Allah's sanctification.

when the season changes,
housewives will run through the streets in daylight
with children glued to their breasts,
suckling pain from their fathers' infidelities and
polygamous pleasures.
they will scream and blame *matikatsi* and *izeqamabhilidi*[1]
for snatching their men away from their families.

hence these women – our mothers, sisters and daughters
will wander the cities in their scarred betrayals,
painting sordid street corners with withered hopes
and wretched wounds dishonouring their minds.
oh when the season changes,
black-veiled widows will resist *ukungenelwa*.[2]
they will strike the rock with spears of integrity and wisdom,
leading them to a wholeness beyond dualities.
revolutionary women will paint their bruised faces
with make-up and red lipstick to disguise the scars of
domestic violence,
while nuns chant masturbation songs and praise celibacy for
delivering them from these social devaluations.

when the season changes,
daughters of Fatima, Jezebel and Maya [3]
will dance to seductive tunes of seven veils –
will belly-dance to free the tiredness from between their thighs;
while others cry in hospital beds, mourning
the removed wombs of their womanhood.

when the season stops changing,
all these diverse women will cram psychiatric wards,
suffering from hysterical destructive thoughts
resulting from daily beatings, infidelity and
foul-mouthed disrespect.
there will be chemical imbalances in our brains
from compromising our values and selves.

mental illness will bloom like spring flowers in our minds,
will enthrall loneliness, in the deepest corners of our hearts, until
we finally stand up and shout:
stop!

I felt tears strolling in my eyes.
I listened to the sound of lies in my ears.
I saw murals of paintings paved beautifully on
the sidewalks of my mind, disordering my thoughts
from sanity.

1. Prostitutes and sluts.
2. It is traditional, when a woman's husband dies, for her in-laws to ask her husband's younger brother to marry her.
3. Fatima – the daughter of Prophet Muhammad; Jezebel – the biblical 'Whore of Babylon'; Maya – the Sanskrit word that symbolises the illusion of material reality in Hindu philosophy.

Judgment day

Khutsang Maroba

From beneath the heels of trampling boots,
I come remolded.
I stand rising with sunbeams from the East,
recovered from the ruins of the West.

I rise never to set,
to retell mistold stories,
rewrite my misspelt name,
sing unsung praises,
mother my orphaned children,
relive my ghosted life.

Ululating, I crush their drums,
chanting to the dance of my own gong.

I go forth on a mission,
my dream reconstructed by a vision.
I summon them boots to a commission
that will end all revisions of me,
seal off omissions for eternity;
today is judgment day.

Me, uncut

Karen Ijumba

I don't dance to your rhythm.
Off beat, my heart beats,
trying to follow your predetermined score,
yet my mind sways from your clearly thought-out plan.

I don't fit into your box,
constricting, restricting, conformity.
I am a circle.

I don't share your vision;
walking vertical on your straight and narrow,
to me, a tightrope.
I'm flying, horizontal, among lazy clouds.

You cannot bash me into your mould.
Ordinary I refuse to be –
a crowd which my face is part of?
No! Stick out like a sore toe I must.
Individual, not fading into backgrounds.

My people's tongue

Bandile Gumbi

I'm on stage mixing fresh tunes
and earth tones
as the theoretical spectacle unfolds
from my lips to kiss the concrete dust.

My people's tongue
My chi
ululates various vibrations
spreading knowledges
beating the madness
that has us all in a seizure.

My people's tongue
My chi
can beat the sense into a stray dog,
sending it home with its tail in the air in pride.

My people's tongue
My chi
can spin a tale on its head
righting a wrong immortalised by ink on paper
sugar-coated for a knowledge-starved child.

My people's tongue
My chi
will wrap you in a cocoon of history
sending your soul on a fantastical journey
to greet your beginnings.

My people's tongue
My chi
has the venom of serpents for every stupidity
which dares to dance on our ancestral graves
behaving in infantile ways.

My people's tongue
My chi
sang a revolution into the heart
of an unyielding mountain,
the songbird carried the tune from tree to forest.

My people's tongue
My chi
dared to enter the den of a lion
and lived to tell the tale-hunters
the truth of what we are.

With my people as my chi,
I stand on a stage mixing fresh tunes
and earth tones
as the theoretical spectacle unfolds
from my lips to kiss the concrete dust.

Iketsetse nnana[1]

Khutsang Maroba

This one is my design,
it won't fit your desire.
It's styled for my curves,
rhymed for my rhythm,
embroidered for my dance.

seka itekanya,[2]
o tla tabola![3]
bona, o a sarolla![4]
ene o tla patala.[5]
jwang o le mohofe?[6]

Too much too little what?
Sleeves are too loose?
Colours just not right?
Keep your two-cents,
come make your own.

seka itekanya,
o tla tabola!
bona, o a sarolla!
ene o tla patala.
jwang o le mohofe?

1. Do it yourself, girl!
2. don't try on the garment,
3. you'll tear it!
4. look, you'll stretch it!
5. and you will pay.
6. how, when you're so poor?

Unshackle the sound

shameeyaa neo waMolefe

farted faeces of urine cologne
have peeped through toilet windows
with warts on the walls,
to recap poets' unaesthetic words.

clichéd performances of those pages
have conveyed ennui, against my ears.
i am drained, tired of hearing the same wretched verses
of complaining protest from passive alcoholic voices
flipping through their pseudo avant-garde theories
on the stages of turban-crowded cafés.

i, through shackles of words
heard caged birds singing,
whistling melodies of jingles and
intruding tunes of *Dhikr** into my silence.
i heard Bheki Mseleku's 'Age of inner knowing'
unchaining emotions and converging the tears on my face.
i felt warmth of oneness in truth with unspoken words and sounds,
conveyed through my ears by his piano rhythms,
urging me to accept, then forgive the mistakes i had made.

journey from within has, through my search for self
allowed me to meet with Allah's senate,
who reminded me of the oneness of life, and
to live in Allah's consciousness by being mistress of my own
universe.

·

through this path, i met acolytes of
Buddha,
Lord Krishna,
Christ, Imam Ali
and Prophet Muhammad (Pbuh)** and his progeny.

i walked these holy sands to celebrate
the gift of light that has illuminated the path.
i walked in praise and thanks
clothing my soul with love, peace and forgiveness in truth.

* Arabic word (usually used by the Shiite Sect) for Allah consciousness or awareness.
** Peace be upon him.

I write to . . .

Hale Tsehlana

I write to untie the knots
that lump my throat
and turn into splitting headaches
when I could simply say fuck off but can't
because I am an African woman
and my mouth must not be foul.
I write to wipe the tears
as the pages of pain
scroll from my thumbs
smudging my mascara.
I write myself into time.
I write that they may know
I became even stronger
when my heart was broken
by culture, church,
civilization
even
syphilization.
I write to share with you the quiet
revolution raging inside my brain.
I write to celebrate my triumph
over poverty, murderers and rapists.
I write to celebrate my self
And lessons learned from the mire.
I write because it is time.

Before poetry was hip

Khanyisile Magubane

Before poetry was hip
we were not gracing stages,
we were going through stages
scribbling on pages
trying to understand these words
that haunted our minds.

Before poetry was hip,
sometimes, sometimes we were too scared
to tell people we were poets,
we did not trust in these words.
Before poetry was hip
we were told to focus on science and accounting,
because words don't put food on the table.

Oh, but they do give peace of mind!

Before poetry was hip
we were an underground people
exchanging words and phrases
stored in files tearing away at the punched holes.

Before poetry was hip
we understood words before we understood love
and the meaning of some of these words.
Sometimes we cut out words and phrases from magazines
and pasted them next to our own written words and
drew funny pictures next to the poems.

Sometimes it was a love poem at 14 – puppy love:
'I love you like the fish loves water, needs water.'
'You are to me what the sun is to a sunflower.'

Before poetry was hip,
sometimes, sometimes we were too scared
to tell people we were wordsmiths,
we did not trust these words.
Before poetry was hip
we could not share these words publicly on a platform.
Voices of criticism are now ears eager to listen –
now we can take ourselves seriously,
now we can just be, just be, just be.
Hip is not bad, indeed hip is not bad.

But long after poetry has lost its shine, has lost its glamour,
we will still be an underground people,
exchanging words and phrases in motions similar to mazes;
but now, we will trust these words,
love these words.

My last poem

shameeyaa neo waMolefe

Intimidated by the spirit of literary forefathers and mothers
these worn-out pens keep flipping timorously
year after day, day after year
to give me the same bluest, blackest and whitest lies.

my so-called muse has finally blocked my creativity
converting it to a writer's block norm.
i am now a jailbird in these dreaded words
an everyday prisoner in this nicotine haze of coffee,
spectacles, dull garments and notebooks
that keep labelling and reclusing me
to sit behind these old bookshelves
searching among them for the rusty voices
that say: *'you have vowed to carry the prickly cross on your back.*
you refuse to be nothing but an "African writer descendent" puppet.
you will continue to scribe where the best minds have blocked.'

my fingers have repeatedly bled bloodied floods
of moody scars onto these blank pages.
these pens have engraved greedy egos
onto my wings
as i drift along smooth sands
where writers of the 20s, 40s, 60s and 70s wait.
with skeptical eyes, they look to us of this generation,
who took an oath in the court of free minds
to ensure that their legacy lives on; they blame us
for these trendy postscript democratic times
that victimise the aesthetics of puns,
syntax and metaphoric phrases.

i am left with subjectivity in my right hand,
writing but hating these now-acclaimed
introspective and illusionary poetic trends
where the jungle connection[1] exploits writing stages with my love.

these maverick eccentric cockroach words of mine
have again undressed my Dadaist[2] nakedness
exposing me before the eyes of these exiled children,
who blame me for not being a proud
'African Renaissance' citizen like them.

the writer's blues have got me caged
in the non-rhythmical tunes of Russian Formalism.[3]
i may be just spliffing[4] my version of truth
in the theatrical stages of my mind.
but the suppressed voices in this poem
have marked it to be the last one written . . .

1. A club in Doornfontein, Johannesburg popular in 2000/1, where poets and writers used to meet to recite and discuss their work.
2. Dadaism was a movement that promoted simplicity in artistic style.
3. Russian Formalism – a literary criticism movement in Russia, which advocated scientific methods for studying poetic language.
4. Slang word for a marijuana joint.

Love

Neiloe Khunyeli

Love is the poem I try for every time I pick up a pen.

I tried to ditch her once, walked
away masking the pain.
Ignored her for a while,
took her off my speed dial.
I said love was played out,
washed up,
done and over,
so very 'last season'.

But because winters flow into spring,
I know love very well.
I dash her with my dreams
ode her with sweet-nothing songs
lyric her in blooms.
Hold her hand in the summer craze
play with her the whole of autumn.
She is the starry tint to my laughter.
My best and only girl.

I love love and love loves me.

So imagine my surprise when she tore
through flesh, got at my heart and squeezed.
And squeezed and squeezed.
Delivered a spasmodic pain to my soul.

I tried easing her out.
Let her blend into the background,
into dim yesterdays.
But that was like walking between raindrops;
Impossible!

Love sought me out,
like a poem that demanded to be recited,
an unceasing resonation of words;
my best and only girl.
Apologies were not even necessary.

Love is the poem I try for, every time I put pen to paper.

My cinnamon

Dineo Luthuli

I cannot stand coffee beans, white pepper,
curry powder, coriander; but cinnamon?
What makes you different?
For only you entice me to leave
my cupboard door ajar.
How can I close it when I can smell
your aromatic arousing scented flesh?
When all I can think about is
your rough yet tender taste against my dry lips?
If I could, I would chew you up until you are inevitably
tenderly ground in my mouth,
on my tongue, against my palette.
If I could, I would swallow you up,
feel you rush down behind my heartburning chest –
if only I could;
my cinnamon.

He held my hand

Khutsang Maroba

A songless soloist,
stumbling up the valley,
dozy, drunk with darkness
he held my hand.

Shook me awake at dawn,
dim eyes despising the worn canvas,
shuffling a scowl;
he held me still.

I watched him with lazy strokes
lighting up the canvas,
my weary eyes widening,
as darkness vanished.

He sang along,
tuning my heart's tempo,
my soul's soothing piano,
as nights of solo ended.

Kisses

Neiloe Khunyeli

You taught me how not to kiss
and tell, how to play the game
slowly folding me into you without
end but speckled with beginnings
of self-hate and full of your
slimy love.

I shut it all out and let you
roam my flesh for satisfaction, I
looked for home in your kisses
riddled with promises you will
never keep.

With a soft kiss you erase the
worn face of a tired wife and I
pucker up to dim her vivid face
from your eyes.

We smooched to feed your old-man's bulge
as you went into me
and I closed my eyes to mute
my disgrace.

Slow and gentle but sometimes
hard and quick with shameful
grunts, a well-kept secret.

My one-way ticket to hell, and
it was always your way, non-
refundable.

A kiss to force your children
out of our corrupted love, kisses
to forget I could be one of them.
Kisses to seal deceit.

Did I ever tell you?

Hale Tsehlana

Did I ever tell you?
That every time you laugh with me,
Warm, invisible fluid fingers
caress and tickle me?

That when I close my eyes in sleep,
I enter the doorway of our past
where you forever beckon me
to come and love you again?

Did I ever tell you?
That your song is my breath of life,
the pulse that keeps me alive?
Your song is a balm,
that bandages my aching heart.

Did I ever tell you?
that your touch, charged with kinetic energy
sends my five senses into a constant orbit?
That your laughter plays hide and seek
on the strings of my soul?

Did I ever tell you?
that your side of the bed
remains unmade since you left?
By the way; did I ever tell you
that I'd marry you again,
if you asked me to?

Could you be more than just my lover?

shameeyaa neo waMolefe

Although we both know that we cannot commit to one another
nor pull strings to sing the songs of oneness together,
I seem always to find myself in bed with you,
freeing myself from myself.

Your sometimes wretched but ecstatic words,
arrogant and subjective phrases,
superficial and intellectual verses,
enlightening and intent lines,
try to impress me but often are obscure in meaning.

I find myself disputing your thoughts,
screaming at your sarcastic syntaxes
that you impose on me.
I dislike it when you hide the sacred silence of truth
deep in the figurative lines you paint in my mind.

Though I like to watch you dance,
undress your nubile innocence and nakedness,
make a fool of yourself
trying to impress me with the books you write,
I still cannot commit myself to you.

Prickly garden

shameeyaa neo waMolefe

The green gestures of the
beautifully planted daffodils and proteas
in your prickly garden
have, over four years, drenched my heart
with the sordidness of your soil.

Your sullen kisses
have, over the seasons
left pungent scents on my lips, and
bitterness on my hips,
as I trace the blurred bruises
of your touches and strokes,
around my curves and thighs.

Tell me;

doesn't the sight and texture
of daffodils and proteas
planted in your prickly garden
over the season, seduce you?

Doesn't the scent and smell
of freshly planted roses and herbs
protected from the blazing sun and
wildest winds, assure you of my love?

Doesn't the sweat of my body, and the
thousand tears cried in the presence
of your nakedness, and
between your sheets, endorse
my sincerity to your garden?

I guess not; for to you . . .

I am a gardener whose poetry and prose
is only worth your insecure interrogation and
non-subjective empirical interpretation
as to why all my poems relate to
experiences before we met.

Listen;

I no longer desire to plant;
nor allow you to walk and play in my garden,
no longer need your insecure touch, your
bitter kiss and fuck.
For it leaves prickles in my heart.

Darling

Khutsang Maroba

I'd rather know no love,
be a stranger to romance,
than live a nightmare
on a weather clock;
cold morning, warm night, rainy day –
what's next?

I sell fish
to build the 'I' dream,
sweat and toil
for my sandcastle
where I'm the only Queen.

If I smell fish . . .
no apologies or compromises;
just *voetstoots,** no guarantees.
Not fitting your size?
Try the next hardware store.

* just as it is.

Eternal

Rose Mokhosi

My spirit lived and soared
through the breath of the universe,
and found me here long before
my mother conceived of me.
Chosen to be born of her, I saw before my time
her fate in the hands of the stars.

Now I too know that little Ayacha already is,
high up in the sky, a moon watching over me.
She waits to be bathed in my womb,
fed through my placenta.
I am humbled to be the one to bring her into life.

She too will tell her own stories
and, perhaps, of the truth about you and I.
Through my pain, she will know of the passion
that was, is, in my being –
that burns in the pit of my stomach.

And when her grandmother smiles upon her,
'Ba re e nere' * she will say;
Ayacha will whisper *'Qoi'*,
And this story, never-ending, will live on.

* A traditional phrase used in Southern Sotho storytelling culture by older women/
  grandmothers when beginning a tale. 'Qoi' is the appropriate response given by their
  young audience.

My heart cries out

Phomelelo Machika

My heart cries out
to wombs that conceive and discard
in the stench of dumping sites,
in airless refuse bags
which cannot sustain life,
breaking ties which would have been.

My heart cries out
in condemnation of hands that receive immaculate life,
rock sickly babies to sleep,
yet still manage to dig worm-infested soil
to conceal deformed babies
who are deemed a curse.

My heart howls at the fathers
who create beauty,
infiltrate its depths, paint it ugly
strand by strand.

My heart cries out
to parents who break the spirit of little girls,
decapitate the childhood of ever-flinching boys
who remain too scarred
to claim their manhood.

My heart still cries out
to those who pass on the seed of self-loathing
which stifles the beat of dreams
hushes the faintest hope;
the seed of hate, which breeds serial killers
creates massacres, and nurtures rapists.

My heart cries out
to those who perpetuate the scourge of poverty
and do not resist the lurking shadow of AIDS.
My heart will continue to sob,
so long as society's ills
fill the morning papers,
find their way to our evening plates.

Little black girl

Rose Mokhosi

Sun-burnt brittle fragile, hair red-braided,
you sit glaring out the bus window,
your small legs afloat off the floor
as you motionlessly stare out at the fast-moving cars.
What do you see abuzz all the traffic?

Cream satin dress, delicate frills on sleeves,
you still sit looking out,
your skinny hands hanging onto the pane,
big eyes reaching into the distance –
a picture so familiar in my mind.

A sad smile, almost sincere, reminding me
of so much pain; the silent cries.
Little black beautiful girl,
with white strap shoes too worn out.
Your innocent gaze moves from the window
to your uncle tom, sitting so close to you.

Your face carries too many questions,
questions I cannot answer – when will we escape?
Like that butterfly fluttering its colourful wings
amidst all the traffic, blessed with freedom,
when will we be free – free from our demons
– our fathers, our uncles?

I wish I could take you home with me,
take you away from this disillusioned
reality you find yourself in.
Rock you gently into a peaceful sleep,
kiss your nightmares away,
see your beautiful smile, hold you in my arms.
And whisper soft words of hope into your tiny ears.

But now, my bus has come to a halt
and I have to jump off.

Cramped streets

shameeyaa neo waMolefe

they walked the streets
with heads bowed low to the ground,
singing penitentiary church hymns
with knives glued to men's heads.

they prostituted their bodies for a living,
bathed their eunuch vaginas on street corners
drenched in the stale semen smells of sex,
waiting for the next clients to service.

they fed their pimps' monologues
on economic justifications,
preaching that the country's currency will rise
with NEPAD, AU and World Summit reveries.*

they traded their communal tribes
for eccentric socialism,
moralised workers' day parades into a disguised secularism.
preached xenophobia with smiling faces
while chanting anthems of the new world order
to the newly acclaimed G8 countries.

they came in masses with destructive wandering minds
to impose their futuristic idealism on individuals.
they snored alongside street vendors, pretending to sleep
while upholding phony images of Dambudzo Marechera,
Ernesto Che Guevara and Frantz Fanon.

they publicly brutalised the game,
governed democracy with monophonic illusions.
played chess and conducted crime from a six-pointed star
dividing up the earth's wealth and scattering currency
to the corners of the six chosen cities.
they traded prostitution with politics, and billed homosexual rights
as cover for less noble agendas.

we fell for the matrix,
rejoiced at the sub-realities lying before our eyes.
we glorified and were secure with our illusions of physical pleasure,
sanctifying power and money in service of men's brutality.
we laughed innocently at '*amapopayi*' ** –
Harry Potter, Pinky and the Brain, Star Trek, Dark Angel,
with *Twelve Monkeys* for fictional fantasy
while we kept asking:
who's the thief behind the crime in the city?

* NEPAD – New Partnership for African Development; AU – African Union.
** Cartoons.

45

The hole I dig for myself

Bulelwa Basse

I'm having a silent nervous
b-r-e-a-k-d-o-w-n

Consumed by the troubles of the world,
as well as my own
I dig myself a grave to lie in,
where I take all the living's aspirations with me.
Dream their successes
Mourn their losses
Cry their tears
Fight for the feeble-minded one's sanity
while I slowly lose mine.

I'm having a silent nervous
b-r-e-a-k-d-o-w-n
is there anyone out there
to SAVE ME?

The forgotten people

Phomelelo Machika

They froze into statistics,
not even seconds after drifting to the other side.
We watch AIDS drain their stamina,
rebuke them for lying passive, like half-burned logs.

We play hosts to this killer
while like termites, it gnaws at the reason
of those dear to us.
I speak of the men and women
who drowned in the air of our ignorance.
I speak for the masses who used to fill our lips,
the voices which broke into laughter
before our very eyes.

I am the voice of the children,
who lost the battle
before they could protest their innocence.

I speak as the coward,
who crouched behind the reeds,
while AIDS carried the mothers and uncles into oblivion.

I appeal to the maternal instinct in you
to bear arms.
I awaken the heroes to raise their shields
against the threat of human breed extinction.

HIV+ by default

Hale Tsehlana

It's not my fault,
yet stigma leeches
onto my brain matter,
reducing me to mere statistics.
Waiting to be born is a pain,
'cause the birth canal ain't right.
I know this passage is my rite,
yet by being born I will surely die.
The dice has been cast
'cause the leeches lurking
in the birth canal
clamour to claim me.
Big brother lies, he says I have
a right to 100 healthy lives.
What's it to him if one more child
is HIV+ by default?
It's not his fault, you see.
People should be
more responsible, he says.
Yet what about me . . . me . . . me . . . ?
Who will speak for me?
Can that be your voice, Woman?

Love immortal

Khutsang Maroba

(In memory of Mamotolo Vilakazi)

I watch her fade away
into the face of creeping dusk.
Slowly swallowing today's beauty,
missing her more every moment,
clasping her soothing hand,
dazed by diamond eyes
beaming, shuttering the twilight.

I feel her moan and groan,
see the soul's agony.
If her load I could only ease,
restore her vigor for a while.
My heart reeling beneath the weight,
her feeble voice urging me on,
we walk the next mile.

Watch the anchors cracking,
sure motions sinking my ship.
Sleepy eyes staring at the monster
wrecking, crushing every anchor.
Like mould devouring best bread
every new dawn claims her share;
dead inside, I detest tomorrow . . .

That endless summer night,
flowers dying on the dinner table,
scents lurking under bed covers.
I'll lean on the windowpane,
wear your winking diamonds,
confide to the soaking pillow,
and wait for our morning.

The children cry

Phomelelo Machika

Playgrounds lie mute,
flaunting rusted desolate swings, too lonely to swing.
Deserted by the familiar tunes
of children playing *black mampatile.**

Children cling onto bed rails,
like mould to tree.
Drowned eyes bulging out from the sea of horror,
deranged by the inexplicable lashes
suffered at the hands of AIDS.

Hope appalled by the sight of children
succumbing to a living death,
failed by those who hold the power to resurrect them.

* hide-and-seek

They sing

Khanyisile Magubane

They sing because they are drunk –
They are, drunk . . .
They drink to forget,
so they remember themselves as young men,
young militant men with vision,
young angry men, hungry for change.

They sing
because they remember
running in the dead of night,
leaving behind loved ones who had already given in,
leaving behind their children
and lovers for the mercy of strange lands.

They returned
and today, as poor men,
the unmentioned but the compensated,
because reconciliation states that 30 thousand rand
per sad story should more than cushion
the effects of their memories,

today
these drunken men entertain us
around fires with their songs, their stories
in musical melancholy.
Their harmonies, their history –
they sing for affirmation among themselves
that they did the right thing (didn't they?)

They still go to bed hungry
because under 'work experience',
they cannot possibly put down: freedom fighter
and under 'reference': my trusted commander,
so they seek distilled counselling everyday.

'Nningasiboni siphuza kangaka, sizama ukukhohlwa.
Ningasiboni sithetha kangaka, sizama ukukhohlwa . . .' *
they would sing.

They sing ultimately because they are drunk,
die hele lot ** – just drunk men.

* 'Don't look at us drinking so much, we are trying to forget.
  Don't mind us talking so much, we are trying to forget.'
** the whole lot.

The place they call home

Phomelelo Machika

The fierce summer heat
swallows the corroded tin houses.
Multitudes sandwiched in squalor
like dead fish in the sea.
Passageways too small
to accommodate the voluptuous African queens.

Debris-filled crevasses.
In the heart of winter's night
fingers of fire sneak up on the cardboard shacks,
then erupt volcanically through the slumbering squatter camps.

Submerged in flames,
the helpless people bleed gushes of shouts
to fire-extinguish cars too lavish
to stroll these streetless cities.

The smell of smoked human flesh
permeates the sullen skies.
Meager possessions dressed in ashes;
the only remnants of a once-vibrant community.

Moses Taiwa Molelekwa

Rose Mokhosi

I remember him, from not so long ago – beautiful black brother, Moses Taiwa Molelekwa. Shy, yet subtly notorious in his own right, I cannot forget him. I remember him from next door, his hair dark and rich as gold – a firm crown on his head. I remember him up on a Broadway stage – features soft as a feather, a smile that almost never faded. And through his love for music, through his music – I have never travelled so much. He took me places near, far and wide – places formerly unknown to me. From the jazzy clubs of New York, through the bright lights of colourful Dubai and back to my roots, our roots – grounding me to our Africa.

A young boy, running barefoot on the dusty roads of his hometown Tembisa, not far from Sophiatown (now called Triomf* – it still amazes me who supposedly triumphed), Moses Taiwa Molelekwa was born a star.

Tonight, like every night, he hits those notes; c-sharp, d-minor, a-lower, over and over again . . . I never want to hear a Beethoven or Mozart! Music of unending intensity, eternal turmoil; he lets me take a peek into his life. All focus is on the black and white keys, his vertebrae so bent his nose almost makes contact with the black head of the piano. The intimate sound of this instrument resonates through his crooked spinal cord, through the nerve endings flowing into and through his heart. Meticulous, this beat-throb is intended to reach my ears' pinnae in the subtlest of vibrations.

* Afrikaans word meaning 'Triumph'.

He lets his fingers just float on the notes – the breeze of the Indian Ocean
– such serenity. My mind at peace. He's almost telling me that he sur-
renders, he acknowledges that he has to breathe easy – that I can breathe
easy. It is amazing the way his music soothes my sometime troubled soul
– and does the same to the soft frown that intermittently emerges from
his forehead.

Just as the quiet wind had seemed to soothe his confusion away, now he
brings in the storm. Slow thunder, swift lightning that threatens to anger
the gods. Like a painter gone beserk, thrusting his brush haphazardly
over the canvass. His movements jerky, he once again bends awkwardly
– slim fingers caressing the keys, his slender body bowed over the grand
piano. Which lets him in, embracing him, so that on that lonely stage,
they seem to bond and fuse into a unison, one being – self-created by
the artist himself.

In climax, he slowly lifts his head and looks into the crowd: 'That's my
life!'

And what a beautiful life, as I applaud this African man who never spoke
much but said everything with his music.

When I heard over the radio that he had taken his life, I sobbed in shock.
I let my tears flow freely for another black soul lost in time – Moses
Taiwa Molelekwa.

I can paint

Khutsang Maroba

Gray-black clouds of malice,
roaring, trembling joyously, glaring
invincible at helpless prey.
Pictures of red oozing rivers,
vibrant, fresh and alive,
sipping, sapping life-springs;
or still, rich brown rot,
reeking, adorned with silky worms,
celebrated by happy vultures.
Round, hollow skulls I can paint,
flawless white fingers clawing at windows,
creaking bones guarding dim corridors.

Yellow tints and blue shades,
waiting for water and paintbrush
one day to balance the equation,
complete the missing lines . . .

Jaded blackness

Neiloe Khunyeli

Peering faces, sick of a notion that defines their very core . . .

It's now cool to be black, flow the flow and tap the funk.
Accusing eyes with one question burning bright, ·

HOW BLACK ARE YOU?

It never stops; once or twice I fell into the blackness and consumed
by the melanin talked Big. When I was young, I used to be slick.
So nowadays lacking the head-wraps and the dreads is two strikes
already – after all, the 'Man' is out to get us. It is slowly coming
back to me, that time when I was once black. Branded a
delinquent by a history that would bind itself to my every
move and every word. Appeared in academic papers
before I even knew what social constructions were.
Whether it was my Grade 12 history teacher or the
world in general, they all told me the same thing:
'This blackness is in you.' And it had a whole
lot of baggage with it.

Always though with accusing eyes, with one question burning bright,

HOW BLACK ARE YOU?

Sure I am the first to admit it, I was once about driving the white folk
into the sea because it sounded good and white is white, right? Damn
the ignorant tags, my history was there in black and white – how were
they going to tell me it never happened? So I was down with the
PAC of the late 1950s and felt I was born after my time a
black panther on the prowl.

Always though with accusing eyes, with one question burning bright,

HOW BLACK ARE YOU?

I still lacked the hair though, and some would say the herb, to get me on top of 'thee world'. I saw all these white liberals, fighting my fight for me. Big ideas and big words, saturated with the big cause. There was a problem and I was it.
Their eyes glistened with freedom and protest marches – damn if daddy saw them on the telly. They cloaked their hearts with this blackness and @ two in the morning over a latte, they insisted it was not pity. Big ideas and big words, saturated with the big cause.

Always though with accusing eyes, with one question burning bright,

HOW BLACK ARE YOU?

So these days it is all about the spoken word. Everybody drops a verse, alienates the *whities* because if you're black you must know. Strange profound lingo, everything rhymes, and who cares what it means because 'boy got style!' He flows better than the Zambezi and is just 'tight' like that. A mini United States saturated with Americanisms. Don't despair, they slur through Jack Daniel-laden tongues, it is still about finding our true selves. Don't be fooled though – you still need to look right and talk right, it is called your right to be insightful.

59

But still with accusing eyes, with one question burning bright,

HOW BLACK ARE YOU?

So when they ask this question, my answer is: NOT BLACK ENOUGH!
I am tired of being the subject of study, debates, hate, love, protest and
drama. I am always in the paper either: raping, murdering, stealing,
tarnishing democracy, getting awards for music, sport or going
outside the norm if I excel academically. They say to wake
up, get dressed, speak, feel, think and drink tea as a black
person – but it is still not enough.

They shout:
be black before you are a woman,
be black before you are a student,
be black before you are a daughter,
be black before you are a Christian.
Just be black before.
So how black am I?

Not black enough I'm afraid, not black enough.

Black and proud

Pumeza Tyoda

I am black and I am proud
Not because the sun is shining outside
Not because it's the 'in thing'
But because my mind, body, soul,
every rib, vein and spirit in me is.
I am black and I am proud
of my past,
for it has brought me thus far –
the no-longer-existent shackles of slavery
and apartheid
have shaped and moulded me into this courageous woman.
I am black and I am proud
of being 'loud', wide and 'round'.
I am black and I am proud
of every extra ounce of weight that bounces
around my African-shaped waistline
every time I move.
I am proud of my stubborn 'kaffir-hare'. *
I am proud of the clicks and twists made by my
tongue and lips when I speak.
I am black and beautiful more within than out.
And as long as the sun shines by day
and the moon at night
I will refuse to preserve my life in a tin
of inferiority complex's
and self-deprecating contexts
but will always stand up for what I am.
For I am black and I am proud.

* 'kaffir-hair'.

What makes me an African?

Pumeza Tyoda

Is it the clicks and twists
made by my tongue
when my language speaks me?

Is it the pigments that colour me black
that make me an African,
or simply being black?

Is it the shape of my body?
the size of my hips, the roundness of my lips
the way I speak or the art of how I sleep?

Is it my name, clan-name, surname
or my hatred for but ownership of a colonial name
as a second identity?
Is it where I come from
where I am or where I'm headed?

Is it the painful history of my fathers?
My present struggle of having to fight
and work ten times harder because I'm black?
And because I'm a woman?
Or the fight for a non-prejudiced future?

What makes me an African?
Sons and daughters of the soil,
enlighten me, let me know.

For the sake of the children I am still to bear,
the stories I have to tell to clarify the myths I've heard
and to clear the confusion in my head.
What makes me an African?
I want to know.

Is it the heroes and heroines
etched on the latest tops I wear?
The scratches that mark my legs
the stubbornness of my head?

Is it the love I share or get?
Is it the wickedness and warmth of my smile?
The way I 'jive'? The drums I play before supper?
Is it colonialism, apartheid or democracy?

What makes me an African?
What makes you an African?
What makes any African, an African?

Let's not pretend

Hale Tsehlana

They put a black father christmas
on some billboard in Bellville,
and said he was black by popular demand!

I dunno who popular demand is,
and frankly, I don't care.

Let's not be abstract
about these things,
we all know that Christmas
in Bellville South and
throughout the Cape Flats,
does not mean red socks
full of chocolate sweets
and goodies under
the special pine tree.

Let's not pretend
that Africa is not too hot
for the steamy christmas pudding
and golden-brown turkey.
Let's not pretend that somewhere
in Bellville, there is
a black father christmas
riding what?
a rickshaw or horse-drawn cart?

Take me back North

Phomelelo Machika

Here, summer pulls a cloth of comfort
over freezing nights
where my rumbling stomach is subtracted,
the breaking dawn like stimulating laughter.

Where mothers spit to make rain
so the children cannot thirst,
where fathers' sweat and vomit provides food
so families cannot hunger.

Where hope suffers no drought
And dreams are irrigated profusely.

Take me back North.
Take me home,
where my people await my arrival.

Her name is Limpopo

Phomelelo Machika

Her tears moisten the throats of victors of war,
yet her eyes itch dry wells of loneliness.
Thinking of deserted fires, night-time stories
which perish untold.
Limpopo, fertile heart.
She gave birth to girls turned too soon into women,
who reproduced a breed
which fills foreign barren lands with fake laughter.

They forget to remember
a lady graceful, woman of many breasts.
She blows life into baobabs, marula even,
whose fruit sustains her strayed children.

Her tongue dances
to the beat of yearning,
blowing her maternal horn,
calling her lost herd back into Africa's Eden.

The pinnacle of my youth

Bulelwa Basse

At the pinnacle of my youth
life stands still,
yet days pass me by . . .

The more my heart walks towards its vision,
the more distorted this vision becomes,
distancing itself from its primal instinct –
to long . . .

Faded ambition, manifests through dreams untold.
Hope evaporated, knows no miracle.
Shackled by fear, talent collects dust.

At the pinnacle of my youth
days pass me by,
yet life stands
still.

Lost

Karen Ijumba

Tears keep painting patterns on my face;
this life, to me, has become a farce –
it's as if I'm alive but not living,
occupying a body simply breathing,
watching as I compromise myself
to make others feel good about themselves.

My life reduced to a game of charades,
like a clown in a circus parade,
acting the fool, wearing a painted smile
yet all the while –
I am strangling my individuality,
suffocating the being inside of me.

The more I squash myself into the social mould,
the soul of my existence grows cold,
my inner self fighting to be released,
depressed into a shrinking verse,
the walls of my self crumbling,
dying,
lost in this rubble of
conformity.

Loneliness

Bandile Gumbi

Restless pent-up energy locked at a place
within this being, which only has a namesake
in vibrating strings brushing a knuckle
while striking a cord in the depth of a moan.
I thought loneliness was a quiet emotion!

The terrain I am travelling is endless and
I'm in never-never land chasing the nothing,
dodging anger, bruising as I trip-fall in my haste;
loneliness is supposed to be a quiet emotion!

The waterfall within is a flooding cataract,
unshed tears pacing up and down
clogging the gorge of my throat.

What a racket! as I swallow this concussion,
a curse, a lump, a teardrop,
while a moan accelerates to overtake.
I blink, pushing the brakes
trying to avoid collision

A SCREAM HITS THE WALL!

Silenced by psychosis and rage

Lisemelo Tlale

So if I have all these dreams and the guts to do anything and everything I desire, why am I sitting on my couch crying like a woman who has just lost a child? I blame it all on a circumstance, of the dramatic kind. I have buried my anger and pain, far too deep. One moment it is *The House of Sand and Fog*, the next it is *Kolya*. When does it end? The forces of nature are at work. The time is right. The context is perfect.

I am scared that someone who did not bring me into this world, is threatening to take me out – without my permission. But is it this that has caused the sudden, almost-violent disturbance in my mind and heart? It is cause and effect. Cause and effect of the Kingsley rendition of my father's road labour and attempted degradation at the hands of pale ignorance. Cause is fear. Effect is betrayal of the lesser kind; perhaps, dancing is my only way out. I told you this was drama!

I scoff down a slice of strawberry cheesecake. I look in the mirror and the flab and anorexic magazine life made me question my Faith. How dare they claim to know about loneliness! I forgive because bitterness does not suit me. But the pent-up energy knocks on my door – this is a desperate need to smash someone's skull in! I should rinse the ring left by shock and age out my cup.

I dress up and fake it like the Conservative Party because the world is still not friendly to single travellers. It was in a fit of rage that I jumped out of a plane at 30 000 ft to feel the forceful wind against my chubby cheeks. While freefalling at a tremendous speed, I held out my hand to my Maker. Back to one of those infamous couch rests, I feel like my world is crumbling – at least I perceive so. Such is drama: Act 1.

I love it when I surpass my petrol attendant's expectations – the look in his eyes knows about compassion. Hence, 'tis not pity.

I love my mother. I love my sister.

I love my brothers. I love my country.

I love the sound of rain against my bedroom window, especially slow rain, on a Sunday morning.

I am in love with my Fate – she gives me reason to live.

The smug Pretenders at work whisper out their own weaknesses. I yell out like the Amazon that I am labelled: 'Race card is not about declared trumps!' They totally disregarded my identity, heritage and pain. They see my mother's boldness as utter disrespect towards the Patriarchy; my siblings and I, on the other hand, see a persistent pioneer who opened not only mental but intellectual doors for us. Hacking away at this negative publicity can be distracting: please remind me to look up to verify my bearings.

These are the smirks of earth after rain downpours, and sun-shiny smiles. They are the smells of hot peanut-butter rye toast and roasted coffee beans – they are safe, they are sane. While my people tend to their crude shelters in the thick of things, the Pretenders flee to their holiday cabins. Yesterday they spat on my great-grandfather. Today he must beg them to reconcile their oppressive falsehoods and pardoned arrogance. When did they ask for forgiveness, granddaddy?

You have to admit, Africa's curves are bewitching. The continent is worth the trouble – I mean the travel.

I bawl my eyes out because I am scared to scream for Help. So help me.

Like a mad woman catching flies in mid-air

Bandile Gumbi

It started on the day when I decided not to come home, not exactly the kind of decision you take sober. It was one drink too many later, when the company of drunken friends made more sense than facing sober parents. I had stepped into a zone of spliffs[1] for breakfast and dinner. Lunchtime was just a moment in the day marked by sunrise and sunset, the kind of stuff middle-class holiday dreams are made of. Those were the days of new beginnings and an end to all my familiars. I was caught in a space where I questioned everything I once thought I knew. No one could blame me if I took due leave of my senses. Since then I have realised that to truly experience change, you have to pass through insanity's door of self-reflection. I can say my journey out of the cocoon of my socialisation was the beginning of my search for my inner truths, some may call independence.

Whenever I walk the city streets I hear a whisper at the corners calling me to strip off my familiar and be naked to the forces that roam the streets, especially after dark. In fear, I recoil like a snake under attack. I always remind myself that no one wants to be a borderline mental case. I say, rather be certified insane, as then you know the colour of your reality because fear is a bloodsucker. On beautiful days when joy is in the warm air we breathe, such thoughts seem to belong in the realm of bad dreams. I will not say nightmares since they are brutal and not easy to forget.

These are the constant thoughts that swirl in my mind as I aimlessly walk the streets of Durban, just connecting with the unfamiliarity of having working hours to myself after a year of employment. The old fears creep in at the oddest moments in the middle of a sea of humanity fulfilling its duties to loved ones and society at large. I'm suddenly in the grip of loneliness and displacement amongst the tall concrete-and-glass office blocks handling humanity behind paperwork until the much anticipated lunchbreak.

I start thinking about my responsibilities as Thamsanqa, second-born daughter without a job, not a victim of teenage pregnancy, educated and still without a plan for my future. I look on as generations of people stream out of office buildings, clutching their five-year plans to status and money tightly under their arms with their newspapers and purses, striding the streets with confidence, as people with clearly marked destinations, I imagine, would do. There is no time to look around and puzzle over facial expressions – time is money. Lunchtime is just about sustenance and running errands, not about finding out what the rest of humanity has been up to while you were locked behind a computer.

I mention my name because it has been both a source of inspiration and a burden for as far back as when I first understood its gendered meaning. I've never thought of myself as extremely 'cultural'; I hardly follow or listen to cultural myths. There is something about my name which does not have much to do with 'luck' (as it means in English). In my culture it is a male name, and I am female. In fact, I have never heard of a female Thamsanqa. Though it is a beautiful name, for a girl grown into a woman, it is a loaded name.

As I was growing up I studied men from afar, in fascination, intrigued, since they were clearly quite a different species from my familiar female-surrounded life. The only man I grew up with is my father. In my pre-teens, when I was still young and innocent, he was the one who would take my friends and me for outings and pick us up from after-school activities: a model dad from the movies. Then adolescence set in on this girl-child and suddenly my understanding father changed to a controlling patriarch. He started infringing on my freedom of movement, using strange excuses like 'girls can't be alone at night'. I would wonder, in utter confusion, whether I wasn't as good and capable, if not better, than the boys roaming the streets at their leisure. After all, am I not Thamsanqa, who is not delimited by the fact that she is born woman? When I reflect on those hectic years, I realise my father had no clue how to deal with raising female children. His own stereotypes about women collided with his ideals about raising independent people. His patriarchal behaviour was a form of protection.

Thus men have always been a curiosity to me, like drugs, with an element of danger and taboo. I guess when an opportunity presents itself, one flirts with danger or simulates it, to acquire the power that taboos, especially dangerous ones, resonate.

I remember the first guy for whom I had sexual feelings. I was jealous of the power he had over me and as a result I found any excuse to beat him up. What attracted me to him was his tall, toned build. He fitted the cliché: tall, dark and handsome. A teenager's fantasy. We took the same lift to school. He liked me, so he let me get away with beating him up and instead of being angry with me, used to buy me chips and cooldrinks. It was really a bizarre situation. I had the power to abuse and I was rewarded for it.

I guess that is why I thought boys were stupid, until I hooked up with two particular girls. They were total radicals in the sense that they aimed to defy the authorities around them; the type of girls who, in high school, formed the nastiest groupies,[2] with their own internal lingo. I call it 'lingo' because I do not think it befits the term 'slang', a term which is respected by some and hated by others. Slang, where I come from, is a generic form of language that is a composition of the languages spoken by people who live in that area and is about preserving, not losing, identity. Groupie lingo does not register on any radar, except in the spaces between the in-group laughs and desires to be a groupie. These girls gave me a different take on this foreign species called 'man'. Apparently males are supposed to be a source of energy. I guess that's why girls can talk about guys 24/7.[3]

The more we talk about them, the more of an energy boost we get. It is a weird sort of chemical balancing, an aspect of science that has never clearly registered on my radar. In my book of life I have ostracised men as energy thieves and a waste of living space, though useful perhaps for procreation purposes. I often ask myself what happened in the beginning of human creation to afford these lucky ones such freedom, whereas I, as a girl-child, should be so restricted. It is a puzzle I am still piecing together, and feminist literature does not give me any satisfactory answers. I resent this lack of knowledge.

In my younger days, I admired boys to the point of wishing I could be one, for no other reason than their freedom of movement. This would mean that I could leave home in the morning and come back the next morning and life would carry on as normal. My mother would then not worry about my safety when I walked around at night, nor whether the neighbourhood would think her child a slut.

The hypocrisies of life are totally amazing, totally dumbfounding to me. In recent times, I have noticed how guys often congregate around one particular guy, who must have some sort of leadership quality. They gather around him and keep him constantly entertained, so enticed are they. The gender gap is always tangibly present in the stillness in the air around them. I have never been welcomed at these gatherings of men. This is a strange phenomenon, because it is not a natural situation as far as I am concerned.

The leader keeps a mental distance from his fans, accepting his so-called 'dues'. I see an ego trip but his 'followers' evidently see a leader. It makes me wonder if, in the end, this revolution (what revolution?) is just about gathering followers, and the real struggle is in the silences, and not the vocal force that has commanded the stage for self-gratification. It finally dawns on me that, in a man's eyes, I am just another woman, with my so-called 'equality' and 'freedom'. My girlfriend Zuziwe used to say: 'Men – it will take a long time for them to overcome the baggage weighing them down to the level of mental slaves.'

In one of my late night wanderings, which lasted a couple of days before I saw the daylight of home, I told this boy-man that I was once confused about my gender identity. I did not mean to actually say it; I surprised myself with my confession. I was naked in truth, to be poetic about my situation. It was an early morning after a good party and a group of friends was sitting in the kitchen. None of us wanted to go home – aside from the fact that I live a bus-ride away and my last bus was at midnight. So you could say we were kind of forced to sleep at the party. I remember taking a snooze on the kitchen table, using Kwazi's thighs as my pillow. When I woke up, Lungi was explaining to a group of guys what it is to be lesbian. We were all friends and fairly comfortable with each other. The alcohol helped to foster the camaraderie. The guys were listening attentively as she explained: 'Guys, it is not like I'm attracted to every woman I see. Thamsanqa is my friend and I love her in that sense but I don't necessarily want to sleep with her.'

Lungi is careful that she does not unnecessarily offend anyone, especially by using blasphemous language; I greatly admire her courtesy. She is one of the few people I know who is in control of her tongue. She is the kind of woman who does a two-step whenever she has a point to make; she punches the air with her voice to make sure the words stick, so that you can never say 'I do not get what you mean'. Just to make sure, she illustrates her points with a joke here, an example there. She plays with your eyes so you can't help but follow her movements. She is a pint-sized drama queen and an amazing dancer. She is a focussed party girl and no man can distract her from the dance floor. Her effect, and the fact that she is aware of it, can lure you to her secret fan club for the naughty and brave.

Anyway, this guy who shall remain anonymous for the time being until I can sort out my feelings for him, turned around and asked 'so are you a lesbian or what?' in a matter-of-fact manner, trying to be off-hand, but not hiding the fascination that most guys feel for two women together. I could almost see him thinking: how do women have sex with each other, how does it work, who is a man and who is a woman? So I answered, 'Honestly speaking, I am confused about this sexuality thing.' I did not elaborate by adding that I am attracted to both men and women, as I normally reply to this sort of question that seems to be asked quite frequently these days. I was taken aback when he asked me to explain myself, and I felt a responsibility to answer him as truthfully as possible for a confused person. I still wonder what he thinks about that whole evening-come-morning. His trying to understand, though, qualifies him as one of the good guys. I appreciate educated black men who can confess to their ignorance.

From that moment I have had the guts to approach the questions life poses less apologetically. I have a tendency to self-reflect around the third month of the year, when it dawns on me that I am well into the new year and there is nothing I can do to change it. This year, what has been uppermost in my mind, is coming to terms with the choices I have made in the past few years, in the hope this will guide me through living this uncertain event – life. I decided that working for a boss should take a minimum of my time. When I look at the number of people who sell their souls to the devil for a job, I feel justified in choosing to step down to give another person a chance to fulfil this ambition. In my own way, I have contributed to the fight against poverty.

This lifestyle has its sobering moments, since you can't live on what feeds the soul through the senses, exclusively. I have a few necessities: art, shelter and food – necessities which are a luxury, since the rand is low. I have also taken a closer look at my social responsibilities, since I am a social being after all. They are always preaching from high platforms (those who are more equal than others) that my country demands my voice. My voice retaliates by shrieking: 'I have the right and responsibility to be who I am – a right that has been denied to many in the socio-political past of our beloved country.'

Those who demand my loyalty promise a bountiful cup of freedom stew, but their words seem to be a lullaby sung to empty spaces. My sanity is challenged at the oddest moments. I have very few political choices and much to fight for, given the strength of an 'I don't care attitude' that has its costs. It makes me think of home, the ideal family that Africans fear and praise, the envy of European individualistic alienation; the one I turn my back on, to chase the voices that promise a life with less responsibility and more freedom from the burden of history. No wonder I find myself prowling these city streets in search of a better reality, free from judgement. I search for my namesake – luck – hoping to bump into her just around that next corner, behind that tree where my brothers prey on others for cents and cheap cellphones.

I take a turn into a street I have not explored before, hoping to bump into inspiration. I pound the tar under the famous African heat, hot and bothered, contemplating whether to vote or not in the upcoming general elections. The ruling party has promised a million jobs in a country where unemployment is so common that it has become an excuse for the lazy. My favourite DJ made a trite but relevant comment the other day: are there a million jobs that are just waiting around for elections? She is a simple woman. I like her, as she always makes this sort of comment. Once, she asked what happens if you find yourself at a tollgate and you do not have money to pay. I have since found out: it is illegal to do a u-turn at a tollgate, and the ladies in those booths are very unfriendly individuals. Their attitude reminds me of my dicey relationship with security guards, who are there to do a specific job, with zero tolerance for unique situations.

I may have an obsessive nature sometimes; I read all those motivational books about soul-searching to find your soulmate. And then I analyse my past relationships. I always try to find 'him' in the person I am with, but the perfectionist in me is never satisfied. As I grow older I try not to strive too much for perfection, but without much luck. It is my de-lusional self-protection mechanism, I guess, because there *is* perfection out there. There must be – unless such a concept does not exist. There surely must be some sort of aesthetic, even if it's only in the mind of the seeker. It is all an illusion anyway, based on some fake romantic notion of what love is, I console myself. Yet this always seems to be disproved by the relationships I find myself in. I tell this to myself without uttering the words to another soul, because in this cynical world, admitting such beliefs would be downright naïve and fantastical. It is stuff for Hollywood B-grade movies, not the thoughts of an intelligent human being. Then I contradict myself and contemplate that fairytales must serve a purpose besides simply entertaining children and filling their heads with mumbo-jumbo (quite a nonsensical word to describe something which must actually exist, otherwise it would not be part of our vocabulary). This is how I feebly indulge myself as I pass the hours between meals and sleep, which eludes me more often than not since I joined the generation of the unemployable.

We live in such contradictory times. I am always struck by that realisation. While my mind is processing all these thoughts, wondering where they come from, my feet are standing at a green robot. It never ceases to amaze me how much of a tragic comedy the streets are, a theatre for poor actors. I am watching a man begging and cursing at the robots opposite me, wearing a cloth like one of those Greek gods. No one is listening or paying heed to his performance. In this city we are not short of public performances: stuff for which we do not have to buy TV licences, nor pay exorbitant movie ticket prices. We are paying for American junk anyway, watching and listening to American mental ills, to imitate and foolishly call 'chic'. These thoughts make me itch with irritation.

1. Marijuana rolled into a cylindrical shape and smoked like a cigarette.
2. A group of people who are followers of a trend or an icon.
3. Twenty-four hours a day, seven days a week; an exaggeration of a constant behaviour.

Poets' Gallery

Bulelwa

Bulelwa 'Midzo' Basse is a 'Slave to Poetry' and National Accounts Manager at C Sport S.A. Born in Johannesburg, she now lives in Cape Town's Langa Township and Bothasig. Her poems have appeared in anthologies published by the Poetry Institute of Africa, in *Angle Search* youth magazine and other forums. She says her inspiration comes from 'the ever-changing life current, its gentle whispers and rude awakenings'.

Karen

Karen Byera Ijumba is 19 years old and a 2nd-year law student at the University of Cape Town. Born in Tanzania, she has been living in South Africa for the past 11 years. 'I began writing poetry in Grade 11 at a time in my life when I was attempting to discover what comprised the substance of my being. For me, writing is more than just an expression of thoughts – through verbalising these thoughts I am able to embark on a journey of self-discovery, self-understanding and eventually self-acceptance.'

Dineo

Dineo Lungile Luthuli is a talented performance poet whose work is a fusion of singing, poetry and conversation. She was a member of the Slang Poets Operation Team (SPOT), a group of poets who travelled around to schools in KwaZulu-Natal promoting poetry, writing and reading to school-children. She lives in Empangeni, where she works at a community centre.

Bandile

Bandile Gumbi holds a BA Social Science degree from the University of Natal (now UKZN) and is studying towards an MA in Communication for Development with Malmo University, Sweden. She has performed at poetry clubs, art exhibitions and creative gatherings country-wide, including the 2004 Poetry Africa Festival in Durban. Her work has appeared in *Agenda* feminist journal and other publications and she has self-published her first poetry collection, *Pangs of Initiation* (2004).

Neiloe

Neiloe Mamokhele Khunyeli was born in Kroonstad in the Free State, 'which I love because it is home'. She has a short story published in *Itch* magazine (2nd Vol.) and is currently working on a novel as part of her MA in Creative Writing at the University of Cape Town. 'I sometimes yearn to say I was born a writer, but in all honesty words found me and I am blessed to have them.'

Phomelelo

Phomelelo Mamampi Machika hails from a village called Ga-Phaahla Mmakadikwe ka di kwa ka di homolela, in Limpopo province. Several of her English poems have been published in *Timbila* and *TurfWrite* poetry journals. She was one of the six featured poets in *Throbbing Ink* (Timbila, 2003) and her Sepedi poetry collection, titled *Peu tsa tokologod* ('Seeds of Freedom') was published by Timbila in 2005. She works as a physiotherapist and continues 'to write about situations past and present which shape who we are as a people'.

Khanyisile

Khanyisile Magubane is a talented writer, poet and journalist who's 'been under the spell of the pen' since she was 13 years old. It was in high school, inspired by her English teacher that she decided to pursue writing as a life-long passion. Khanyisile is an English Literature and Communication Studies graduate, with an Honours degree in Journalism. She's been a radio journalist for the past six years but recently resigned to pursue a full-time writing career. She lives in Randburg, Johannesburg.

Neo

shameeyaa neo waMolefe is 'a writer and avid reader, passionate about gender, esoteric and political issues'. Born in Transkei, she lives in Soweto, Gauteng and is employed by the Independent Communications Authority of South Africa (Icasa). She is also studying towards a degree in Human and Social Sciences, specialising in International Relations and Diplomacy. Her literary work has been published in *So Much to Tell*, Vol. 1 (Women in Writing, 2003); *Educational Practice*, Issue 3 (Gauteng Department of Education, 1999); and on the Internet website, *Kush Kollective*.

Hale

Hale Tsehlana is a lecturer in the English Department at Stellenbosch University. She enjoys travelling, music and art in all its forms – including an occasional 'karaoke swing'. Her interests revolve around creative writing and its use in academic development. Her poems have been featured in various journals, magazines and Internet sites. The highlight of her 'poetic career' was a sponsored trip to sing praises to the Himalayan Mountains. Her first poetry collection: *Poems and Songs from the Mire*, will be launched by New Voices Publishing in 2006.

Khutsang

Khutsang Maroba grew up in QwaQwa in the Free State but is now based in Pretoria, where she works as an Accountant. She started writing poetry while studying at University of the North, 'encouraged and coached by my English lecturer and a close friend who is an acclaimed poet. My poetry is a story of the various experiences at different stages in my life, which many young women can identify themselves with'.

Lisemelo

Lisemelo Tlale is currently based in England, working, travelling and writing. She has a B.Com in Economics and Business Information Systems. Several of her poems have been published in *Botsotso* and other magazines, as well as in anthologies such as *isis x* (Botsotso, 2005). She also has a poetry collection at the National English Literary Museum (NELM) in Grahamstown. 'I continue to write and hope to publish short stories and a book some day. Life is so much better when I stop to smell the flowers.'

Pumeza

Pumeza Tyoda was born in Butterworth in the Eastern Cape and is currently a student at University of the Western Cape (UWC). She occasionally performs at UWC poetry events and is a member of the Cape Peninsula University of Technology (CPUT) Poetry Society.

Rose

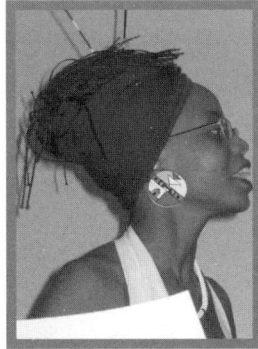

Rose Mokhosi was born in the Free State but relocated to KwaZulu-Natal, which she considers 'home'. She recently joined the Centre for Creative Arts at the University of KwaZulu-Natal as a literature festival co-ordinator. She says: 'I am inspired by life, and everything around me. I write when inspired – and I believe in women empowerment and upliftment. We are the pillars of our society – AMANDL'EMBOKODWE!'